THEN AND THERE SERIES
GENERAL EDITOR
MARJORIE REEVES

Learning and Teaching in Victorian Times

AN ELEMENTARY SCHOOL IN 1888

SECOND EDITION

P. F. SPEED, MA

Illustrated from contemporary sources

LONGMAN

LONGMAN GROUP LIMITED
*Longman House, Burnt Mill, Harlow, Essex CM20 2JE, England
and Associated Companies throughout the World*

© P.F. Speed 1964
Second edition © Longman Group Limited 1983

First published 1964
Second edition 1983

ISBN 0 582 22107 2

Set in 11/12½ Baskerville, Linotron 202

*Printed in Singapore by
Four Strong Printing Company*

Contents

To the Reader

All the facts given in this book are true. All the events took place. Moreover, they are things which could easily have happened to your own great-grandparents. This is not a book about great men. It is, in the main, about an ordinary school, with ordinary children and teachers, in an uneventful year, 1888. When you have read it, I hope you will be able to imagine yourself back in 1888 at a school like the one I am going to describe.

However, because this book is about ordinary people, it does not mean that its story is unimportant. For centuries most of the children of England had gone without an education. Then, between 1800 and 1900, it became possible for almost every child to go to school. This was a revolution which completely changed the life of this country.

You will notice a few words printed in *italics*. You can find out what they mean in the Glossary on page 93.

1 The Building

Where did your great-grandparents go to school? It is quite likely that you could find out, and when you have done so, perhaps you could go and visit the building. It is very likely that it is still standing and possibly it is still used as a school. While you are there, try to imagine what schooldays were like for your great-grandparents – the gloomy old place will certainly help you to do this.

To help your imagination you should ask any old people you know to tell you all they can about their childhood days. Listen to them carefully and make notes of what they say. You will then be able to compare the information they give you with what you will find in this book.

Here you are going to read mainly about a school in Campbell Square, Northampton. This was a 'public elementary school'. The word 'elementary' is difficult to explain. It really means the beginning stages of learning, and certainly this school did only simple work, but so did many other schools which were not called elementary. However, if you used the words 'elementary school' in 1888, people would think not so much of the work done as the kind of child that attended. Elementary schools were for children whose parents were not rich. Many, indeed, were very poor.

In those days schools for poor children were often in bad buildings and Campbell Square School was no exception. Like so many others it was near the middle of the town, and built right on the street. Here people gathered to gossip and argue, traders were noisy, and horses and carts made a terrible clatter. Today schools can be built on the outskirts of cities, but this was hardly possible in the 1880s. Why not?

Above: *Campbell Square School, Northampton, in 1888*
Below: *A plan of Campbell Square School in the 1880s*

	BOYS' LAVATORIES	GIRLS' LAVATORIES	
CLASSROOM			CLASSROOM
CLASSROOM			CLASSROOM

BOYS' SCHOOL ROOM	HEADMASTER'S HOUSE	GIRLS' SCHOOL ROOM
ENTRANCE		ENTRANCE

The picture opposite gives you a good idea of the size of the school and what it looked like.

The plan of Campbell Square School changed a good deal as time went on. Today it is very difficult to work out what it was like originally, but it must have been something like the plan at the foot of the page opposite.

The School Room was once one big room. It had been the only teaching room in the school, but by 1888 it had been divided by a wooden screen to make two classrooms. Other classrooms had also been built on at the end.

Inside, the building was gloomy. The window-sills were so high that it was impossible to see anything but the sky. The lower part of the walls was covered with dark-brown boards, and the plaster above these was whitewashed. The whitewash rapidly went grubby, and tended to flake off.

Such heat as they had came from open fires or stoves. This was all very well for the teacher, who could put himself where he wanted, but the children were not so lucky. Those near the fire were roasted, and those away from it were cold. One winter day the headmaster noted in his *log-book*:

> The cold weather this week has interfered with work. The scholars' fingers have been so cold that they could not produce good written work. Two boys were sent home in a fainting condition.

The teachers had trouble getting enough fresh air. Not all children in those days washed regularly. The noise from the street made it impossible to open the windows. So what could be done to prevent the room getting smelly? One answer was to make the rooms very high, which they did by not putting a ceiling under the roof. But this left many ugly beams on show. Another thing was to put *louvers* on the roof. The wind passing through these drew stale air from the classrooms. Naturally the amount of fresh air depended on the strength of the wind.

7

Children warming themselves by a school stove. Can you think of any disadvantages of heating a classroom with a stove?

Furniture was simple. There were blackboards and easels, shelves and cupboards. The teacher sat at a desk on a tall chair so that he could see all over the classroom. The children did not have separate desks and chairs. They sat on benches, about eight on each, and both the bench and the desk were fixed to the ground. This meant that tall children, short children, and medium-sized children all sat at exactly the same distance from their work. Moreover, if you sat in the middle of a row, you could not get out without disturbing your neighbours.

The lavatories were dreadful. In many schools they were just a row of seats over an open drain. The boys had to flush this themselves by pouring buckets of water along it. By 1888

Campbell Square had a more advanced kind of lavatory pan. It was flushed by pulling a plug on the end of a rod, in much the same way as you empty a bath. Unfortunately the plug had a habit of sticking.

Children playing in a school playground in the nineteenth century. Do you recognise any of the games?

Finally, I must tell you about playgrounds. Many of the older schools had none, though Campbell Square did. It was, however, surrounded by a wall which was so high that it made the place look like the exercise yard of a prison. There were no playing fields.

Of course, bad buildings do not matter too much as long as the teachers are good. Unfortunately, when your great-grandparents were at school, good teachers were few and far between.

2 The Teachers

If you were able to go back and meet the teachers of Campbell Square School in 1888, you would find them different in many ways from the teachers at your own school today. One of the most surprising things, however, would be the age of the younger members of the staff.

First, you might see John Spencer. He is just twelve years old. He is a *monitor*, and his wages are £6 a year. Every *quarter-day* he gets a postal order for thirty shillings (£1.50). John thinks it is a long time to wait, and it is not much when it comes. His friends in the factories earn much more.

When Campbell Square School opened in 1812, monitors did all the teaching, with the headmaster supervising them. John is thankful that those days have gone, and it is not often that he has to take a class on his own. This only happens when one of the older teachers is absent. On a normal day John helps Mr Beal with his class. He gives out the slates, pens, pencils, books and paper, rings the school bell and watches the children as they move in and out of the classroom. Often Mr Beal teaches a small group of boys round his desk, and then John keeps an eye on the rest of the class to see that they carry on with their writing and do not talk or get into mischief.

John's parents are keen for him to become a teacher when he is grown up, but he has already had enough of school. He thinks that being a teacher is even worse than being a pupil, and he is determined to leave as soon as he can.

Next you should meet William Foster. William is fourteen. He started as a monitor like John, and when he was thirteen

MONITOR'S

CLASS BOOK

ON

NATURAL HISTORY,

BY

THOMAS HALLIWELL,

BRITISH SCHOOL, MARSDEN.

1848.

BURNLEY:

PRINTED BY J. CLEGG, DUGDALE'S BUILDINGS.

8

This great family is divided into four Classes:—

1. *Mammalia*, or Mammiferous Animals.
2. *Aves*, or Birds.
3. *Reptilia*, or Reptiles.
4. *Pisces*, or Fishes.

The first of these classes is the most interesting; it comprehends those Animals whose organization is most developed, whose senses are the most delicate, whose intelligence is the most perfect, who are intimately connected with ourselves, who possess most of our attention, and are more essential to our immediate welfare, comprehending Man himself.

To the beings which belong to this class, our observation will be exclusively confined; as the class Mammalia (and it is the case throughout every other) contains groups of Animals, which present common agreements in form and structure, and common dissimilarities from other groups, we are led naturally as it were, or by an involuntary operation of the mind, to institute a series of sections, in each of which, those Animals are thrown together which have a mutual resemblance to each other in certain prominent characteristics.

These sections are termed orders; the following Table exhibits the arrangements of CUVIER, and most Naturalists of the present day, and is that which is universally received,

Monitor. How is the Animal Kingdom divided?
Describe back-boned Animals,
How divided?
Describe soft or pulpy Animals,
Describe jointed Animals,
How divided?
Describe rayed or branched Animals,
How divided?
What do you remark on the covering of different Animals?
Give the Classical name of each Sub-kingdome.
Give their derivations.

A monitor's class book on natural history. Can you work out how the monitor would use the book?

---

he signed on as a pupil teacher for five years. At first his wages were £15, but they go up by £3 each year. He now has £18, or £4 10s (£4.50) each quarter-day.

Pupil teachers were often called apprentices. An apprentice spends part of his time doing the easier jobs in a trade, and part of his time learning from the older craftsmen. This is what William does. During the day he helps one of the older teachers, and during the evening he has lessons from the headmaster. Much of his work in the day is like a monitor's but, unlike a monitor, he sometimes has to take charge of a group of boys and teach them. Sometimes, indeed, he finds he has a class of over sixty. It is difficult to keep them 11 under control, and even more difficult to make them learn anything.

The classroom is overcrowded, many of the children are dirty and badly behaved, and by the end of the afternoon William feels he has had as much as he can stand. His work, however, is not over. After a short break he and the other pupil teachers have to go to the headmaster. The headmaster is kind enough, but he too has had a hard day, and is often impatient and irritable at the end of it. Now he has to prepare his pupil teachers for their examinations. They learn many of the subjects that you learn today in a secondary school – English, Mathematics, History, Geography and Drawing. In addition, they have to study books on the art of teaching, and William finds these very hard to understand.

Unfortunately, William is not a satisfactory pupil teacher. He is often late for school, and he has other faults too. Here are some of the complaints the headmaster made about him:

> Foster allowed his boys to sit idle in the classroom for thirty-five minutes.

> A mother complained that Foster had been striking his boys in the classroom with a strap.

> Foster reading a tale from a *penny miscellany* this afternoon instead of attending to his class. The other teachers are doing their best, but Foster, from his carelessness and *indifference*, requires much more looking after and gives more trouble than any pupil teacher I have ever had.

In case you should think all pupil teachers were like William Foster, you had better meet Samuel Campion.

Samuel is in the fifth and last year of his apprenticeship. His salary is £27 a year. He is nearly nineteen years old, and has been teaching for so long that he is efficient. The children do not like him. They think that he is conceited and that he throws his weight about too much, but not many of them dare to play him up. The headmaster is pleased with Samuel's progress. This is what he once wrote about him:

12

This afternoon a lesson was given by Campion on the silk worm. The matter was carefully arranged and mastered by the teacher, delivered in a lively style and illustrated with numerous specimens.

Although Samuel is developing into quite a good teacher, he is rather worried about his own studies. At the end of the year he will have to go to London to take an examination called the Queen's Scholarship. If he passes it with a first class, he will be able to go on to a *training college*. If he gets a second or third class, he will be able to come back to Campbell Square as an assistant master. If he should fail, however, he would have to remain a pupil teacher and try again the following year. This would be a blow to his pride.

The next teacher you should meet is Thomas Beal. He is twenty years old. He was once a pupil teacher in the school, but as he passed his Queen's Scholarship, he became an assistant master. This was a big step up. In the first place, he got a rise in salary and now earns £60 a year. He is no longer called by his Christian name, like monitors and pupil teachers. The headmaster calls him 'Mr Beal' and the boys are supposed to call him 'Sir'.

Although he has finished his apprenticeship, his studies are not over. He is now working for his *Certificate*. Other men are studying for this full-time at training colleges, but Thomas Beal was not lucky enough to win a place at college. All his studies have to be done in his spare time, and he finds it difficult to settle down to his books after a hard day at school. However, he feels it is all worthwhile, for if he gets his Certificate he will at once receive an increase in salary. He also knows that without the Certificate he will never be able to become a headmaster.

Thomas Beal was a pupil at Campbell Square, then a monitor, then a pupil teacher, and is now an assistant master. He has not been to a secondary school, nor has he been to college, and so he has not had a very wide education. As a result his teaching is dull and boring. Moreover, he treats the 13

Teacher's Certificate.

Certificates are of four classes. — No Certificate is issued above the fourth class. Certificates are raised to the higher classes by good service only. — The fourth (lowest) class consists of an upper and lower grade. Teachers in the lower grade of the fourth class are not recognized for the superintendence of Pupil Teachers, until they have risen to a higher grade either by re-examination or good service.

The Committee of the Privy Council on Education

Hereby Certify That, in the month of December, 1869,
James Jones having been a Student during
completed an years — the engagement as Pupil Teacher satisfactorily in — was examined before
Her Majesty's Inspector of Schools, and placed according to the order of Proficiency in
the third Division of candidates of the same standing

Also That in the month of May 1870, the above named
candidate after having been employed for 2 1/12 years in the Liverpool St. Paul's National
School was required to teach a class in the presence of Her Majesty's Inspector of Schools,
who made the following Report.

"Jones has an active manner; he keeps a class quiet and attentive,
with satisfactory results as to the children's knowledge of the lesson"

(signed) H. Hughes H. M. Inspector

In order that this Certificate may serve as evidence not only of attainments and skill,
but also of practical success, it may after each period of five years be revised according
to the number dates and character of the Inspector's entries upon it. No Teacher
who has changed more than once from one School to another during the five years preceding
Revision can be raised to a higher class.

W. E. Forster
Vice President

children harshly, as he is, secretly, rather afraid of his class. Thomas Beal is not popular with his pupils. Even the headmaster does not think too highly of him, as you can see from this entry in the school's log-book:

> T.C. Beal, assistant master, has been late on several occasions during the last fortnight and was thirty minutes late again this afternoon, causing great *inconvenience*.

He is wearing a bandage, for he fell off a form a few days ago and cut his head. The boys were delighted.

A more popular assistant master is Mr Covington. He is twenty-four years old; he has a Certificate and so he is fully qualified. His salary is £85 a year and as he is a single man he is quite well off.

The headmaster is pleased with Mr Covington, for he works hard and his discipline is good. The boys like him, too, for, although he can be stern with them, he is usually kind and is always fair. He is also a good teacher and his pupils learn much from him.

Everyone feels that Mr Covington has a bright future ahead of him.

It is now time to meet the headmaster. In Victorian times this could be quite terrifying.

In 1888 the headmaster of Campbell Square School was Mr Alfred Jones. With a salary of £250 a year he is one of the best-paid teachers in Northampton. In those days £250 was a lot of money. He went to a training college as a young man and, when he took his Certificate, was placed in the first division of the first class. He is a kindly man, who believes in keeping order without being too severe. When he came to the school he tried to do without the cane altogether, and succeeded for six weeks. But it was all spoilt by some boys who, as he put it, 'mistook the spirit in which I acted and compelled me to use it. I did so with *salutary* results'. He found it paid to be firm as well as kind. He describes what happened when a boy had played truant several times:

> After *admonishing* him I have punished him in the usual way, namely with three stripes with the cane on each hand.

However, he always hates punishing boys, unlike some teachers who seem to enjoy it.

He is sympathetic to boys who are in trouble. Once a lad ran a pen into his own eye when he was looking into his desk

A Victorian headmaster – Henry Hackwood

and Mr Jones raised the money for him to go to London to see a specialist. He also likes to see boys enjoying themselves. He noted in his log-book, 'weather severe; good slides in the playground'.

Moreover, so that they could have fun all the year round, 16   he had a slide, some swings and some vaulting bars put up in the school yard. The boys were very pleased with these. Being in Mr Jones's class is not too bad at all, as long as you behave yourself.

However, in case you should think all teachers of this time were as pleasant as Mr Jones, you had better read this description of a master who was then teaching in the West of England:

> Mr Wadsworth had a fine head and a really handsome *profile* which, terminating in a long beard and surmounted by his *skull-cap*, made his figure one not easily shut from memory. He was a very fair *disciplinarian*, but in his administration of punishment he exercised his powers in two ways which were unwise. First, he would flick a scholar's ear with his second finger smartly released from the thumb, a means of punishment which, after a proper amount of practice, is calculated to inflict a much greater consternation and suffering than might be casually supposed. The second, and still more objectionable, form of punishment of which he was fond, consisted of seizing two boys by the right and left ears and bumping their heads together with considerable violence. It never paid to attempt to avoid Mr Wadsworth's canings and the boy who withdrew his hand lived to regret his timidity. Mr Wadsworth would hold his finger-tips in a vice-like grip and add *substantial interest* to the contemplated punishment.

In the end, this teacher was forced to retire because his right arm became paralysed!

You may like to know what happened to these people in later life. The monitor, John Spencer, defied his parents and refused to sign on as a pupil teacher. He left school when he was thirteen. The pupil teacher, William Foster, developed *consumption* and had to give up his job. The managers gave him £5 when he left, but this was indeed a sad ending to an unhappy career.

Samuel Campion, the other pupil teacher, passed his 17

Queen's Scholarship, but not well enough to win a place at college. He came back to Campbell Square as an assistant master and began to study for his Certificate in his spare time. However, he found the work too difficult, so he gave up teaching and went to work for a local newspaper, the 'Northampton Herald'.

I do not know what became of Thomas Beal, but you can read what happened to the other assistant in Alfred Jones's own words:

Funeral of Mr Covington at which the teachers of the school and the scholars of the class attended as a last sad expression of their sorrow at the loss of a colleague and friend whom they much respected and loved.

The only happy ending was for Alfred Jones. You will read more about him at the end of this book.

3 The Classes

Campbell Square School, like any other elementary school, was divided into standards. The lowest of these was Standard I, and the highest was Standard VII. Most of the children in Standard I would be seven or eight years old, and if all went well they would move up one standard every year. This would mean that the children in Standard VII were thirteen or fourteen years old.

To move from one standard to another you had to pass an examination that was conducted each year by an inspector. If you passed, you moved up; if you failed, you had to stay where you were and try again when the inspector arrived the following year. Of course, there were a few children who kept on failing and some indeed spent their entire school life in Standard I. You can imagine how boys of twelve felt, having to sit with children of seven and eight. It is one of the reasons why so many of the older, backward pupils were unwilling to go to school.

What happened if a child, instead of being backward, was particularly bright? There was nothing to prevent a pupil missing a standard or even two. The teacher could present children for examination in any standard he chose, and, if he felt that a boy of eight could pass Standard III, that boy would sit the examination with Standard III. If successful, he would go up into Standard IV, where he would find himself working with children three years older. Unfortunately I have no figures for Campbell Square School, but the table on the next page shows what it was like in the *British School* at Bath.

			STANDARD				
AGE	I	II	III	IV	V	VI	VII
8	65	23	2	2			
9	9	26	33	3			
10	2	6	15	29	5		
11		1	12	29	32	1	
12	1		2	6	15	12	2
13			1	2	13	14	10
14					2	5	3
15				1		1	
TOTALS	77	56	65	72	67	33	15

Study the table for yourself and find the answers to the following questions:

What were the ages of the youngest and the oldest children in Standard IV?
What was the average age of this standard?
How many children had been kept down in Standard I?

There is a further question you should ask yourself. Why are Standards VI and VII so much smaller than any of the others? You should know one reason for this already, and you will find another when you have read Chapter 5 on Attendance.

To sum up, we can say that children of average ability were in the correct standard for their age. Those who were backward were kept down; those who were bright were pushed ahead.

Think about the differences between the old school and those today. How does your own school treat children of different abilities? Do you think that this arrangement is any better? Do you think children of different abilities should have different treatment? In your discussion of these points, it might help you to find out what they do in the United States.

A class in Bristol in 1895.

THE SIZE OF CLASSES

How many pupils are there in your class? How many are there in the biggest class in your school? How many are there in the smallest? What is the average size for a class? When you have these figures for your own school you can compare them with the numbers in classes in for Campbell Square in 1888:

Largest class 90
Smallest class 68
Average class 78

Look at the photograph of a class in a Victorian school. Guess how many children there were in this class. Remember that not all the children can be seen. What problems would a teacher have with a class of this size?

21

4 The Children

Three old gentlemen, all of whom were boys at school in the 1880s, have told me about their lives in those days. They are Edmund Biggs, Frank Jones and William Drage.

EDMUND BIGGS

Edmund's family was not poor. His father was a cabinet maker and his mother kept a guest house. There were four

A family taking its Sunday walk. The man on the right is the vicar

boys in the family. The parents were kind, but they were also very religious.

Sunday was a dreadful day for the boys. It began at eight o'clock when they came down with their shoes shining and their hair smelling of oil. After breakfast they went to Sunday school, and after Sunday school to church. Before dinner the whole family went for a walk. This was to see their neighbours' Sunday clothes and to show off their own. Opposite is a picture of a family out for a Sunday walk, having a conversation with the vicar.

The boys had to leave off their cloth caps and instead wore bowler hats, which they found rather uncomfortable. After the walk came dinner, and after dinner, Sunday school again. Then they might escape the grown-ups for an hour or two, but they had to be careful. They could read religious papers like 'Sunday at Home', but if their parents caught them with their comics they were in trouble. In the evening they went to church again and, when they came back, their father read them the Bible until it was time for bed.

You will understand that these boys wished to enjoy themselves for the rest of the week. Sometimes their parents took them to the theatre and once a week they went to dancing classes. They enjoyed their own amusements. They liked going for long walks and, later, to his great delight, Edmund's parents gave him a bicycle – a brand-new machine of the latest design, known as a safety bicycle. Otherwise they might play games like marbles, buttons, tops, hoops, cricket and football. On page 24 you can see some boys playing marbles.

All this was harmless enough, but they found amusements of another kind. Gangs from rival schools would gather in the streets and have battles. There were no tomatoes to throw in those days, but they did very well with potatoes, eggs, sticks and stones. Sometimes they would follow the lamplighter, putting out the gas lamps as soon as he had lit them; they would tie string to door-knockers and bang them from a safe distance; they painted railings and statues; they bombarded pedestrians. Drunkards gave them a lot of fun. Some of those wretched people would lie down in the street to sleep and the boys tickled them in the face with a feather tied on a stick.

Children playing marbles

But not everything was fun. Edmund had sometimes to go to the dentist, and his parents could not afford to pay for *anaesthetics*.

Edmund had also to go to school. He disliked it, since he was a lively boy and objected to the severe discipline. His parents, however, stood for no nonsense and he attended regularly. As a result he made good progress. Moreover, he stayed at school until he was thirteen and had passed Standard VII. When he left school, he got a job in an office and, later on, he did well in business.

FRANK JONES

Frank's parents were not rich. His father was a labourer, but
he worked hard, never smoked and never drank anything

except a little beer. Money was often short, but Frank and his brothers were never without food.

The boys played in the streets and, although they were sometimes a nuisance, they seem to have kept out of the mischief done by the Biggs brothers. Frank remembers the Sunday school more kindly than Edmund. He recalls that there was an annual Sunday school treat. The teachers would take the children into the park, where they organised games and gave them each a bun and a mug of lemonade.

With this family, the only real trouble came when someone was ill. The parents could not afford proper medical care, and although it was sometimes possible to have free treatment at the hospital, the doctors did not care about the poorer patients. Frank Jones still remembers the screams that came from the dentist's cubicle.

Like Edmund, Frank attended school regularly, and, since he was a bright lad, he got on well. However, as his parents were not well off, he left school to work as an errand boy as soon as he had passed Standard V. By then he could read and write very well and was quick at figures, though he had not had enough education to do as well as Edmund.

WILLIAM DRAGE

William's father was a tiler. He was also a man of original ideas. When the chimney wanted sweeping, he used to fire his gun up it, with blank ammunition. The whole house seemed to shake and the soot came tumbling down. He had no alarm clock to wake his children in the morning, so he used to kick a bucket down the stairs.

It was a large family and they were poor. The father worked hard enough, but there were many children to feed and he was sometimes out of work. On those days he would often go into the country with his gun, and, if he was lucky, would bring home enough rabbits or pigeons to make dinner. Often William had to stay away from school to earn money, and he left school without learning to read or write. Families were often too poor for the children to have a proper education. 25

A family of beggars

There were, however, plenty who were worse off than William Drage. Some of the children from very poor homes led unhappy lives. There were parents who got some strange satisfaction from being cruel. A father might beat his child with a stick, a strap or his fists for little reason, or no reason at all.

Some people trained their children to be criminals. They would send them out to steal from shops or pick pockets, and thrash them if they came home without enough money. There were also children who were made to beg. In winter they would go out into the cold wearing just a few rags and with sore places rubbed up and inflamed in order to make people sorry for them. You can see a picture of a group of beggars above.

Some parents even turned their children out of the house altogether so that they had to live where they could find shelter, under bridges, in timber yards, or in the market. Dr Barnardo found many such homeless children in London and this was why he started his homes.

The number of children deliberately ill treated in these ways was not as great as the number of children who were simply neglected. However, neglect can be just as cruel. Many poor folk lived in such miserable houses that they had to get drunk to escape. This, of course, only made things worse, especially for the children. Here is a description of a home in which the mother was a drunkard.

> The room was in a dirty and stinking condition; the children were huddled round a fireplace with no fire in it. They were clad in rags which were not sufficient for warmth, and these rags were covered with vermin as were their heads. There were also a number of sores over their bodies. The bed was black with dirt, and was made of rotten flocks. There was a sheet and a blanket in the same state covered with a filthy piece of carpet.

Poor children were badly clothed. This cartoon from Punch will help you remember that they had no shoes.

An unfortunate handstand!
'– and, it is not a Pleasant Thing, when going out to Dinner, to have a Summersault turned on to your Stom — we mean Waistcoat.'

Left: *A poor and homeless street urchin*
Right: *The same boy transformed – living and working in a home run by Dr Barnado*

Here is a description of a little boy found wandering in the streets of London; it is from a book called 'London Labour and London Poor' by Henry Mayhew. It was written in 1851, but there were still plenty of children like this in 1888:

Mike wore no shoes, but his feet were as black as if cased in gloves with short fingers. His coat had been a man's and the tails reached to his ankles; one of the sleeves was missing and a dirty rag had been wound round his arm in its stead. His hair spread about like a tuft of grass where a rabbit has been squatting.

28　The picture above on the left is of just such a boy.

The dirt and bad clothing were a nuisance at school. You can imagine what the smell was like when large numbers of children arrived wet from the rain and crowded together in the classrooms.

With bad clothing went bad food and bad health. Children had skin diseases like *ringworm* and *eczema*: bad feeding made their bones weak so that they grew up deformed; damp and poor clothing helped to cause lung diseases. Many had fleas and lice.

Since their homes were so bad many such children chose to spend most of their time in the streets. Here they might find some amusements.

The water-cart

You will know some of their games – marbles, cricket, football, with sliding and snowballing when the weather was right. Others are less common today. Hoops were favourites with the boys and they often got into trouble, bowling them along crowded pavements. In the summer the water-carts were fun. The streets did not have the hard top which we know today. The metal tyres of the vehicles ground the surface into a fine powder. On hot dry days, the water-cart went round to lay the dust. It worked like a huge watering can and the children liked to run behind it getting a free shower-bath.

A few boys followed their parents into the public-houses. There was no law to prevent this and before long the children were going there of their own accord.

This entry is in the log-book of a school at Bruton in Somerset:

> In the afternoon the boy Sheen was absent and stated to be in a public-house, drunk. Reported it to Mr Randolph who, with the Revd J White, found it was too true.

For most of the time, however, children in the streets were not enjoying themselves, but were trying to earn money. In your other history books you will have read about children working in factories. This went on even in 1888, but it was carefully controlled. There were plenty of ways of making children work, apart from sending them into factories. This table will give you some idea of the work done by children in their spare time out of school. You can work out how much they earned in an hour:

CHILD	OCCUPATION	HOURS PER WEEK	WEEKLY WAGE
Girl, aged 11	Minding a baby	27½	6d(2½p)
Girl, aged 8	Errands	11½	4d(1½p)
Boy, aged 12	Newsboy	31	2s 6d(12½p)
Boy, aged 12	Errands	22	2s 0d(10p)
Boy, aged 10	Errands	27	9d(4p)

Children who worked such long hours could not learn much at school, even if they attended regularly, which they did not do.

You will have read enough by now to realise that the children at an elementary school came from very different kinds of homes. Some were very poor, the children of neglectful or cruel parents. There was very little the school could do for them. There were others, like William Drage, whose parents did their best, but were defeated because their families were too big and they could barely earn enough to feed them.

A crossing sweeper. Many children worked as crossing sweepers. Why do you think they were needed?

Here again, the children had little benefit from going to school. Some, like Frank Jones and Edmund Biggs, were luckier. Their parents were good to them, even though they were severe. Children from homes like theirs could learn much at school.

Campbell Square was fortunate in that many of its pupils came from good homes. Some 'old boys' did very well in later life. Indeed, when he retired in 1914, Alfred Jones claimed he had caned more Mayors of Northampton than any other teacher in the town!

31

5 Attendance

It was a long time before Parliament decided to make all children go to school. The Education Act of 1870 gave *School Boards* power to make education *compulsory* in their own areas, if they wished to do so. Northampton decided to do this in 1873. Later, two Acts, taken together, made education compulsory all over England. We name them after the politicians responsible for them. They were Lord Sandon's Act of 1876 and Mundella's Act of 1880.

As a result of these Acts, most children had to attend school until they were thirteen, but there were important exceptions. First, children over the age of ten could leave school if they had passed Standard V. Secondly, children who had passed Standard IV need only attend school two hours a day, if they were over ten. You can imagine how annoyed teachers were to lose a good number of their pupils two hours after school began. Alfred Jones said they should stay at least until the end of morning school. He got into trouble with the boys' employers for keeping them.

It was, however, one thing to say that children must attend school; it was quite another to make sure that the law was obeyed. Many children were bad at attending school.

Often children were absent because something exciting was happening in town. Here are some of the entries from Alfred Jones's log-book:

Northampton Races. Very thin school.
St George's Fair. Thin attendance.
Small attendance – military review.
Soldier's funeral – thin school in consequence.

A more serious reason for absence was bad health. As you have seen, many children were underfed and unhealthy, which meant they were often unfit for school. There were also epidemics. They had measles, as we have today, but there were other diseases that were more serious, like scarlet fever. These entries from Alfred Jones's log-book tell their own story:

> I have had a greater number of cases of small pox reported this week than I have had since Christmas and several deaths.

> The fear of small pox on the one hand, of compulsory *vaccination* on the other has reduced attendance considerably.

Sometimes parents were hard-up and needed the money their children could earn. For many years, this was the main reason for bad attendance at school – parents were unable or unwilling to do without their children's wages.

These children look as though they are up to something!

One boy who often stayed away from school was William Drage. You already know something about him. He told me why he did not go to school more often than he could help, and his reason was quite simple. He did not like school. He did not like being caned on the hand, still less did he like being bent over a desk and thrashed. He did not like the way some of the young assistant teachers threw their weight about. William found the lessons difficult, not because he was stupid, but because he missed so much through absence. The headmaster caned him when he played truant, but he preferred to put up with that and have his day of freedom, rather than come to school.

When he was older he stayed away to earn money for the rest of the family. His parents were fined, but as he earned far more money than they had to pay in fines, they thought it was worth it. He left school a year earlier than he should have done.

The results of not attending school were sometimes serious. William Drage could not read or write when he left school and had to teach himself. He was able to do this, but a great many were not.

Moreover, children who were not at school were often running round the streets learning bad habits. One headmaster wrote:

> The many who attend badly figure during school or after life in the police court. One of our old truants was charged this week with stealing whisky, claret and bottled ale from the racecourse. It is always found that boys who attend badly and during absence receive the education of the streets, have a bad influence on the tone of the school.

Bad attendance also meant that schools got less money from the government. Every year the government gave quite a lot of money to the school as you will see on page 73. These grants depended to a considerable extent on the average attendance and Alfred Jones once complained bitterly:

Attendance this week is only 66, that is, 211 less than last week in consequence of the Races. The loss of grant on average attendance will be more than the school fees for the week.

The teachers did what they could to make the children attend school regularly. The simplest way was to cane the truants. Alfred Jones did this a lot at one time. He gave it up because he thought that it was hardly fair. He felt, rightly, that the parents were often more to blame than the children.

Another thing that could be done was to give prizes to children who attended regularly. Some schools gave handsome certificates like the one below. One gave medals. Each medal had on it a picture of an *hour-glass* with wings and over it the words, 'Delay not. Time flies!' Most children did not much care whether or not they got one of these. On page 36 you can see a photograph of children who were 'Never Absent' from school in one year.

What reward for good attendance is shown on this certificate?

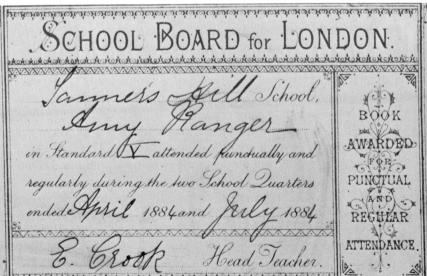

Children from Whalley National School who were 'Never Absent' from school for one year

The School Boards had the main duty of seeing that children went to school. They drew up a list of rules, or bye-laws as they were called, and appointed some attendance officers. These men inspected the registers of the schools and, if they saw that a child was frequently away, they would call on the parents to ask the reason. This could be a dangerous job and sometimes attendance officers had a rough time. If the parents refused to send the child to school, the School Board might have them summonsed. Even if the Board brought the offenders to court, the magistrate would often let them off with no more than a small fine or a warning. The result was that parents were not afraid at all of being summonsed. One man with a large family was fined seventy-two times.

It is easy to see why the magistrates were not more strict. They knew how poor many people were, and how much they needed the few shillings a week that their children could earn. When men were unemployed, the children had to find jobs or the family starved. As one magistrate said: 'There are more important interests than education. People must live.'

6 The Lessons

If you had been at school in 1888, I do not think you would have liked the lessons. One reason was that few teachers ever tried to make the work enjoyable. A book of hints for teachers said:

> Every child should understand there is a time for play and a time for work. Every minute of time in school must be spent in work.

The writer felt that if a child enjoyed his lessons, there was something wrong with the teaching. Many agreed with him.

You will be able to think of other reasons why lessons were not enjoyable, if you remember what you read about some of the younger teachers, the crowded classrooms, and the unruly children. When schools were like this the only way to keep control was to see that all the children in the room did the same thing at the same time.

They moved about the school as if they were a squad of soldiers doing drill. One old gentleman told me how it used to happen in the British School at Bath. The boys all came in from the playground in single file, singing a marching song so that they kept in step. They had five songs, one for each day of the week. The headmaster stood at the door beating time on the ground with his walking-stick, and if he wanted them to hurry up, he increased the beat, so that the march became a trot. Once inside, the boys sat in their desks singing until everyone was in his place. Then the headmaster blew a mighty blast on his whistle and the singing stopped, often right in the middle of a verse. The desks were of the   37 old-fashioned kind, and it was almost impossible to stand comfortably in them. The problem was how to bring all the boys out of their desks for prayers. They did it like this: from the centre of the schoolroom the headmaster called, 'Desks, turn!' At this strange command each lad stood, turned to the right and placed his left hand on his own desk and his right hand on the desk behind. Then came the command, 'Out!' and five hundred boys vaulted over the seats of their desks and landed on the ground with an enormous bang. After prayers the headmaster ordered, 'Desks, turn! In!' and the boys vaulted back in the same way.

Instruction for small groups at Boy's Home, Regents Park Road in 1870. Why are there two teachers? Who do you think is the boy on the left, facing the class?

Even lessons were rather like drill. The teacher would order, 'Open your copy books! Take up your pens! Copy this sentence on the board! Put down your pens! Close your books!' – and so on. Any boy who failed to keep up with the rest found himself in trouble.

Pictures of Victorian classes usually show the children packed together in perfectly straight rows, looking far too scared to move a centimetre without an order from the teacher.

What is it like in your own school? Do you think you get enough freedom, or too much?

One serious problem of the big classes was that a teacher could very rarely help individual pupils with their own particular difficulties. The best that could be done would be to tell a group of children to come out for questioning, while the remainder did some writing or some silent reading. You can see a group of children being taught in this way in the picture on the opposite page.

It is now time to look at some of the subjects which were taught.

If you were asked what was the most important subject you were taught at school, what would you reply? During the last century, most people would have answered without hesitation that it was religion.

The kind of religion your great-grandparents were taught depended upon the kind of school they attended. Many schools belonged to the Church of England, and so they taught the religion of the Church of England. A very important part was the *Catechism*. If you do not know what the Catechism is, you can find it in a Prayer Book.

Board Schools and British Schools were different from Church Schools, as neither belonged to any particular church. Consequently they both taught *non-denominational religion*.

How does all this compare with what happens in your own school today? What is your own religion? Is it taught in the school you attend? Do you go to a school which belongs to the Church of England or the Roman Catholic Church? If not, do you know of any such schools? If you are friendly 39 with any of the children who go to such schools, ask them about their lessons in religion, and compare them with those given in your own school.

With religion went lessons on good behaviour. Alfred Jones's log-book shows you what happened:

> A visitor gave a most interesting address on the importance of education, perseverance and temperance.

> Lecture on '*Total Abstinence*'.

> Mr Finnemore of the National Temperance Society gave his lecture on 'Alcoholic Drinks are not Foods'.

An even more unusual entry comes from the log-book of a school at Bath:

> The following Societies were started by the Master:

> THE TEMPERANCE SOCIETY. Scholars who join this promise to abstain from all intoxicating liquors.

> THE MISSIONARY SOCIETY. A meeting lasting not more than five minutes is held on the last Friday in each month. A short address is given. Pence are collected for their coloured brethren across the seas.

> THE PURE WORD SOCIETY. All who join this promise to use no bad language, to refrain from harsh words, to speak kindly to all with whom they come in contact. This is worked by the boys themselves and names of offenders are entered upon the Black List.

Next in importance to religion came elementary subjects. These were reading, writing and arithmetic, usually called the 'Three R's'.

Children learning to read started with the letters. They went on to easy passages and then more difficult ones until, in Standard VI, they were expected to read Shakespeare, Milton and other such authors. At the beginning of the century, schools used reading sheets. By 1888 a child was normally given a reader. Nonetheless he would only have one

A page from 'A New Introduction to Reading', published in 1808. The book was intended for six to twelve-year-olds

Easy Lessons of Words not exceeding Two Syllables.

Lesson I.

A GOOD name is better than precious ointment; and the day of one's death than the day of one's birth. It is better to go to the house of mourning than the house of feasting; for that is the end of all men, and the living will lay it to his heart. Sorrow is better than laughter; for by the sadness of the looks the heart is made better. The heart of the wise is in the house of mourning, but the heart of fools is in the house of mirth. It is better to hear the rebuke of the wise, than for a man to hear the songs of fools.

Lesson II.

DID youth know the pleasure that arises from an early culture of the mind, I am led to believe they would never waste in useless pursuits the many hours that are done that way, when to their sad regret they will sooner or later find their mistake in the end.

How many have I been witness to, who would have given life almost to redeem mis-spent time, when they have seen others

of

Below: *Two pages from an alphabet book*

book until he went up into the next Standard. If he finished the book before he was due to go up, he read it over again. Some children went through their books so often that they learnt them by heart. We even hear of children repeating accurately a whole page for an inspector, holding the book upside-down!

Here are some passages from a Standard I reader:

> The birds are at rest in the trees. See how each one hides its head in its wings. It is time too, for you to say 'Good night', and go to bed. But do not go to rest till you have knelt down to pray to God and to thank Him for all His love and care!

> She went up to the cage with some nice seed to give to it. But the poor bird lay dead in the cage. It had died for want of food. Oh, what pain it must have felt! Boys and girls, keep this sad tale in your minds and be kind to your pets.

Did you notice two things about these passages?

In the first place you can see that the book is trying to teach not only reading, but also religion and good behaviour. The whole book is full of little moral tales.

The second thing about these passages is that no word is more than one syllable. Check this for yourself. You will see that the author even wrote 'till' instead of 'until'. Is it true that young children find one-syllable words easy? Up to a point they do. For example, 'sad', 'cat' and 'big' are easy, because if you sound the letters you make the sound of the word. But what about 'mean', 'true' and 'pain'? What happens if you try to sound these letter by letter? Short words are often very difficult. A poor reader will have trouble with 'head', 'bead' and 'dead' because all three look alike but are not all pronounced the same way. Longer words are often easier, especially if they stand for something nice or exciting. Children can usually read 'chocolate' and I have never met a single one that could not read 'mother'.

In the readers for the older children the words are longer and the passages more difficult to understand. Now and then there is something exciting like 'Rounding Cape Horn' or the 'Prairie On Fire'. However, there are still many pieces about religion and most of them make gloomy reading.

One story is called 'Death of Little Nell'. It is taken from a book by Charles Dickens called 'The Old Curiosity Shop'. Each paragraph begins, 'She was dead', except the last one which begins, 'She had been dead three days.' There is also 'The Wreck of the Hesperus', which you may know. It describes how a little girl was drowned at sea. Another poem has, as far as I know, been long since forgotten. It began:

> The night was dark and stormy,
> The wind was blowing wild.
> A patient mother knelt beside
> The deathbed of her child.

Children learning to write started on slates. This picture shows where they were kept. Slates had one advantage – they

Boy putting away his slate

could be used over and over again, saving the expense of paper. Slates had many disadvantages. How do you suppose the writing was rubbed out? Good little children brought with them a damp sponge, but most of them forgot, so they cleaned their slates with what was known as 'spit and shirt-cuff'. Also slate pencils make dreadful squeaks if you hold them in a certain way, and some children did this on purpose. Finally, slates were dangerous weapons. Many a teacher had to dodge a flying slate as he chased a disobedient pupil from the classroom. All in all, it was a relief when children went over to paper work, which they did in the upper standards.

The favourite style of handwriting was *copper-plate*. Here is an example of this writing:

Good handwriting is essential

In the days before typewriters, good handwriting was very important, especially for boys who wanted jobs in offices. You will see that the copper-plate is as easy to read as print, and many people think it is beautiful.

Children had to learn how to spell. The teacher would put a list of words on the board and the class would all chant together, 'F-a-i-t-h, faith, f-u-l, ful, faithful'. Older children might have spelling books. These books gave lists of words, grouped together in various ways. They might start with one-syllable words – 'sprain, strain, sail' – and work up to something really ambitious – 'experimental, labiodental, antipestilential'.

What did they write? They did very little that was interesting or exciting. First, they had their copy-books, in which, as the name suggests, they copied work from the blackboard or from a book. It was no more than an exercise in handwriting, and what they wrote might not even make much sense. One exercise was to copy out:

Cork is the bark of a very large tree,
Cockles come from the deep blue sea.

Copy-books were supposed to be perfectly neat. We still have a proverb about copy-books – an expression which means to make a dreadful mistake. What is it?

For the rest, the junior standards only had dictation, Standard I, single words, and the others, easy sentences. Standard V went one step farther. They first listened to a passage and then re-wrote it in their own words. Only Standards V and VI wrote regular compositions, using ideas of their own.

In arithmetic Standard I had to learn their numbers up to 1,000, do easy sums in addition, subtraction and multiplication, and learn their tables up to twelve times six. Standard II had to do division and Standard III, money sums. By the time they were in Standard VI, they were doing fractions, decimals, simple proportion and simple interest.

An arithmetic lesson

Do you think the course in arithmetic looks very difficult? Remember that division was started in Standard II. How old were most of the children in this class? Having worked this out, try to discover when children start division in the primary and infant schools in your own neighbourhood. You could also check when they learn their six times table.

The arithmetic was not always well taught. The young assistants and pupil teachers were not very good at helping their pupils think for themselves, so many children never really understood what they were doing.

Some teachers even tried to introduce religion into the arithmetic. This is easy enough in a reading or writing lesson, but whatever is religious arithmetic? They set problems such as:

'Abraham had 750 sheep and Lot had 533 sheep. How many did they have together?'

They might also have a rhyme like this, which was supposed to teach morals as well as arithmetic:

Two pints will make one quart,
Four quarts one gallon strong.
Some drink too little, some too much,
To drink too much is wrong.

The main work of the elementary schools was to teach the Three R's. However, most schools did more, for the Government encouraged them to teach what were known as 'class subjects'. If they taught them properly, they might earn a bigger grant. If the Government had not offered a grant, it is unlikely that the teachers would have taken these subjects very seriously. Alfred Jones showed quite clearly his real interest in teaching history when he wrote in his log-book:

Made arrangements for a more systematic teaching of history with a view to obtaining an extra grant for it.

No school was compelled to take 'class subjects', but, if it did so, the Government said that it had to teach English grammar. This amused some people. They were quite sure that learning English grammar would never teach children to speak correctly. One School Board member in Somerset quoted a local rhyme:

Us will not go back for she,
For her does not belong to we.

Children at Alfred Jones's school would say 'Om got', for 'I have' and 'He's coom', for 'He has come'. Is there a special way of speaking in your area? Do you think that schools should encourage children to drop it? Do you imagine that learning English grammar helps children to speak English more correctly?

13
Contd.

extent, the *Emperor of Russia*, and the *Sultan of Turkey*. Despotic monarchs vary in the power they exercise.

A *Limited* or *Constitutional Monarch* rules after certain fixed plans, and the laws of the country are made and administered by a body of men called the *Legislature*, chosen by the people for that purpose, as in *England*.

RELIGIONS.

14
1. The **Religions** of the world are often classed under two heads—

Mono-theistic, or the worship of one God, and

Poly-theistic, or the worship of more than one God.

2. There are *three chief divisions* of Mono-theistic Religions—the Christian, Jewish, and Mahommedan.

The **Christian Religion** generally prevails in Europe and those parts of the world colonised by Europeans ; such as the countries of *North* and *South America, Australia, South Africa*, and *New Zealand*.

The **Jewish Religion**, which had its origin in Palestine, is still the religion of the Jews wherever they are found.

The **Mahommedan Religion** prevails in *Turkey, Northern Africa*, and *Western Asia*, that is west of the Ganges basin.

The most prominent forms of **Poly-theistic** Religions are the various kinds of *Fetichism* prevailing among some of the natives of *Africa* and the islands of the *Pacific Ocean*.[1]

QUESTIONS.

1. Of what does the surface of the Earth consist, *and in what proportions?*

2. What are the largest divisions of the Earth called ?

3. How many continents are there ?

4. What is meant by the Old World and the New World ?

5. What is Oceania ?

6. What are Continents divided into ?

7. Explain the meaning of the terms *island, peninsula, isthmus, cape*, and *coast*.

8. What are volcanoes, and what prevails in their neighbourhood ?

9. Define the terms *plain, plateau*, and *valley*.

10. What are the largest divisions of water called ? Name them *and give their positions*.

11. Define the terms *sea, gulf, bay, bight, strait, channel, lake*, and *river*.

12. What is meant by the *basin* of a river, and the *water-shed* of a country ?

13. What is the estimated population of the world ?

14. How many races are there ?

15. Write out a description of each race.

16. What is the difference between an absolute and a limited monarch ?

[1] Though various idols are worshipped by the *Buddhists* of China, Further India, and Thibet, and by the *Brahmins* of India, they are regarded as emblems of Deity. The *Parsees*, too, adore the sun, as emblematic of the Deity.

THE UNITED KINGDOM.

15
1. The **United Kingdom** is situated on the West side of Europe, in the Atlantic Ocean, and consists of *Great Britain* and *Ireland*, with the adjacent islands.

The **area** of the United Kingdom is somewhat more than **121,000 square miles**, or nearly **one-thirtieth** part of the entire area of Europe ; whilst its population is nearly **41½ millions**,[1] or about **one-ninth** part of that of Europe.

2. **Great Britain** is the largest *island* of Europe, and consists of *England*, in the South ; *Scotland*, in the North ; and *Wales*, west of England.

3. **Ireland** is an *island*, separated from England by the *Irish Sea* and *St. George's Channel*.

Ireland was conquered by England in the reign of Henry II. 1172 ; but Henry VIII. was the first English sovereign styled " *King of Ireland*"—his predecessors being called " *Lords of Ireland.*" The Parliaments of Great Britain and Ireland were not united until the time of George III, 1801.

Wales was conquered by Edward I., but was not incorporated with England until the time of Henry VIII., 1536.

Scotland was united to England in 1603, when James VI. of Scotland, being heir to the English throne, became James I. of England. The *Parliaments* of England and Scotland, however, were not united until the time of Queen Anne, 1707.

4. **England** is the *largest, wealthiest*, and *most populous* portion of Great Britain.

London, the Capital of England, is also the *Capital* of the **British Empire**, which consists of the *United Kingdom*, her *Colonies, Dependencies, Protectorates* and *British India*.

[1] In 1901 the population was 41,454,621. England and Wales, 32,526,075 ; Scotland, 4,472,000 ; Ireland, 4,456,546.

A geography text-book published in 1902. How is this different from a geography book today?

Teachers had a wide choice for a second class subject if they wanted to take one. Usually they would choose the kind of thing that you learn in your own school – geography, history, geometry, algebra, science or even a foreign language.

A common subject was geography, which today most children seem to enjoy. You learn about different countries, their 47 climate, their rivers and mountains, and you see how these things affect the lives of their people. You are encouraged to think for yourself, and you can illustrate your note-books with maps, diagrams and pictures. In Victorian times however, children simply learned facts by heart. Some of the exercises were to learn the rivers of the British Isles, in their order around the coast, the railway stations on the line from London to Holyhead, the names of the Channel Islands, and so on.

Most schools could not find the time to teach any more than two class subjects, and so there were plenty of children who hardly touched history, algebra, geometry or science. Campbell Square School was an exception. Alfred Jones experimented with several subjects. He even taught French for a while, which was most unusual in an elementary school, but it cannot have been a success, as he gave it up after three years.

Most children learnt singing, and this was also a grant-earning subject. For learning songs by heart and singing them by ear, each child could earn sixpence (2½p) a year for his school. If he could recognise the musical notes, written on the stave, and sing them, he earned a shilling (5p). Here Alfred Jones was a pioneer, for it was he who first used the *Tonic Sol-Fa* system in Northampton.

With such large classes, it was almost impossible to teach children musical instruments. They had very few chances for hearing good music, properly played. Why was this?

Not many schools could afford a piano. To give the children the right note to start a song, the teacher had to use a *tuning fork*, or, failing that, to sing the note himself.

Science was not generally taught, but they did have something like it in object lessons.

In 1888 object lessons did not earn grant, so teachers only gave them occasionally. But they were good practice for pupil teachers. This is the way an object lesson should go, according to one book on how to teach. This lesson is on a 'Piece of clay'.

Show one of the lumps of dry clay.

'Who can tell me what this is?' 'It is a piece of clay.' 'Where did it come from?' 'It was dug out of the ground.'

'All have seen clay turned up wherever any digging is going on, for it is found almost anywhere.'

Make the class tell where they have met with clay.

'We have a common name for all substances which we get out of the earth in this way. *We call them minerals. Clay is a mineral.*'

Break up the lump into small pieces and distribute round the class. Set the children to examine them and make them tell what they can about this substance.

'How easily I broke the lump into small pieces with my fingers.'

An object lesson for a class in 1898. What object is the class studying?

A science lesson at a school in London in 1897

Let them dig pieces out with their fingers and nails, with their pencils, or with a knife.

'What does this teach us about the clay? It is soft. *We call clay a soft mineral.*'

Give the children some pieces of moist clay, and set them to make some common things. First let them make a brick, then break their brick and flatten their clay into a sort of plate. Let the plate pass into a basin, the basin into a flower-pot and so on, the teacher taking up the task where individuals fail.

Teachers did not try to teach a proper science like physics, chemistry or biology. Instead, the children studied an extraordinary mixture of objects. The object lessons given at Campbell Square School, at various times, included the silk loom, iron and its manufacture, blood and its circulation, elephants, shape and motion of the earth, gold, sugar, and camels.

The only practical subject that boys learned was drawing. There was no woodwork, metalwork, craft or gardening. You will note, too, that it was not 'art'; but 'drawing'. Art involves the use of the imagination, and that was about the last thing a child needed in a drawing lesson a hundred years ago.

You will understand this if you look at some of the drawings that children were expected to do. Here is a beginner's exercise:

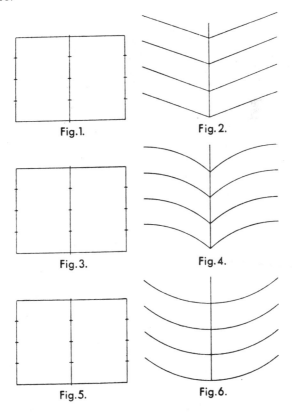

Fig.1.   Fig. 2.

Fig.3.   Fig. 4.

Fig.5.   Fig.6.

Do you see the point of Figures 1, 3 and 5?

On the next page is a drawing of average difficulty.

Finally, on page 53 is a drawing from the end of the book.

Children did not always copy diagrams; they might draw objects. Most schools kept models of cubes, cones, spheres and cylinders and the pupils first learned to draw these. Later, they went on to 'common objects' – such as buckets, jugs, books or cases. The children were never allowed to make up their own pictures.

PE was just military drill. The purpose of drill was not so much to keep the children fit, as to help with the discipline of the school. Teachers imagined that the children would learn habits of obedience from moving promptly to commands given on the parade ground.

At Campbell Square School, this lesson was taken by a retired soldier, Colour Sergeant Culverhouse. He drilled the boys in exactly the same way that he had once drilled squads of recruits. Anything less like a modern PE lesson it would be hard to imagine. There was one similarity. Then, as now,

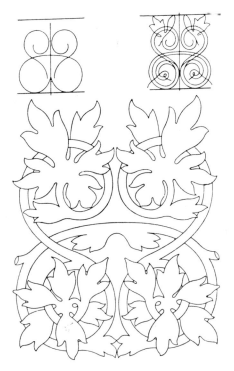

there were children who dodged the lesson if they had the chance. Alfred Jones entered in his log-book:

> The boys generally like the drill, but one has already asked to be excused on account of the *fatigue*.

No one today – either teachers or children – would like to return to these old-fashioned ways of teaching.

We have seen that Victorian children spent too much time in the classroom. Classwork is very important, but it needs to be balanced by practical work and by physical education.

The classwork was usually dull and uninteresting. The main trouble here was that so many of the teachers were young and inexperienced and did not know how to make lessons interesting.

The children were rarely encouraged to develop their own ideas, to think for themselves, or to use their imagination.

A school leaving certificate. Can you see the school motto at the top? What do you think it means?

When Victorian children left school they were given a School Leaving Certificate. Whose certificate was this? At what age did he leave school? What subjects did he study at school?

7 Girls' and Infants' Schools

Girls who have been reading this book may want to know how their great-grandmothers were educated.

Buildings were the same as in the boys' schools. Classes, too, were the same, as the girls had to go through the same standards. There were, however, even fewer girls than boys in the higher standards. Attendance, too, was poor.

Girls, you may agree, are generally better behaved than boys and they did not play truant so often. They frequently stayed away, however, to help in the home. Mothers found their older daughters much too useful to send them to school! Teachers, too, were much the same as in the boys' schools, except that they were girls and women. There were monitors, pupil teachers, assistants, and headmistresses. The headmistresses were often very stern.

You can see that the headmistress of Campbell Square School was severe from these extracts in her log-book:

> Two girls caned today – one for telling a lie and taking what was not her own, the other for persistent idleness and carelessness.

> Three girls caned for sliding in the infants' playground and coming late in consequence, also one child for playing truant and one for persistently coming to school at ten o'clock without excuse.

> Several girls caned for careless work.

Do you think the headmistress was right to cane the girls for all these offences? Do you think she should have given some other punishment for some of them? Do you think girls should be caned at all?

You may know, from other history books, that Victorian girls and women had nothing like the same freedom as those of today. They were not even expected to think too much for themselves. They had to be guided by their fathers when they were young and by their husbands when they married. They were to be good mothers and housewives, and to be dutiful and obedient to their menfolk, and that was all. A piece of advice to a young girl was, 'be good, sweet maid, and let who can be clever'. You may have also heard the saying, 'A woman's place is in the home'. Most Victorians believed this very strongly. How do you suppose all this affected girls' education?

To a certain point girls learnt the same things as boys, and in much the same way. They had religion, reading, writing and arithmetic. These four subjects took up most of their time. They also had some physical exercise. On the opposite page there is a picture of a girls' class doing drill.

Most girls' schools taught drawing, mainly to earn a small extra grant. There were few other subjects for girls. They probably had a little English literature and grammar. Even this annoyed some people. One member of the School Board complained bitterly that it was a waste of time to teach grammar to girls. How could grammar help them to become good housewives? He said, 'they could better spend their time learning how to darn stockings, to mend clothes or to do some other domestic duty.'

As you can see, the girls received the same education as the boys, but cut down to suit people who were never to have to think for themselves!

In one way, however, the girls were luckier than the boys. They were expected to become good housewives so they had a fair amount of practical work.

The first kind of housecraft introduced into the elementary schools was 'plain needlework'. This came in 1862, when the Government made it a compulsory subject for girls.

Physical Education at a girls' school. PE was usually called 'Drill'. Can you think why?

Here is a list of sewing materials at one school:

Sewing Cotton, Wool, Calico, Stocking Web, Java Canvas, Holland, Linen, Tape, Lining, Flannel, Baize, Binding, Thread, Darning Cotton, Print, Muslin, Flannelette, Linen Buttons, Trimmings, Silesia, Yosemite, Cambric, Lawn, Huckaback, Zephyr, and Saxony Cloth.

Here is a list of the things made at the same school:

Knitted Cuffs, Socks, Chemises, Drawers, Aprons, Babies' Nightdresses, Frocks and Skirts, Pinafores, Print Aprons, Knitted Vests, Glass Cloths and Dusters, Kitchen Towels, Dishcloths, Flannel and Knitted Petticoats, Overalls, Nightdresses, Handkerchiefs, Bodices, Boys' Shirts, Flannel Petticoats.

Needlework was the favourite housecraft subject and for a very good reason. It was cheap to teach. It could be taught in an ordinary classroom and the school could recover some of the cost of the material by selling the finished articles to the girls who made them.

Other kinds of housecraft were not taught in Northampton in 1888. Cooking, you will agree, was a very important subject for girls, but it does need a special room and expensive equipment. When, finally, they began to teach cookery, School Boards usually set up centres. These were special rooms for cookery, often in technical colleges, and the various schools sent their girls to the centre in turn. It also meant that very few girls from each school could attend. It is quite a modern idea that each school should have its own domestic science room.

It is also a modern idea that girls should have the same chance of a good education as boys.

INFANTS' SCHOOLS

Generally infants' school were brighter and happier places than the schools for older children. For this there were two reasons. In the first place many people were beginning to take notice of the work of two men, a Swiss named Pestalozzi, and a German named Froebel. Both had written books on the education of young children and although many of their ideas were very difficult to understand, one or two things were quite clear. Above all, they said that children should be brought up in happy surroundings, with plenty of interesting games and toys.

The other thing that made life easier, was that the infants did not have to pass any examinations set by the Government inspector. The inspector came every year, and if his report was good enough the Government gave the school a grant. But the grant did not depend on how many passes the children won in an examination. This was a big relief for teachers and children.

This is not to say that everything was perfect. Infants'

Infants playing with their teacher, 1908. Look at the clothes worn by the children and teacher. What game do you think they are playing?

schools still employed too many monitors, as their salaries were the lowest of all. Monitors were often thoughtless, unkind and inefficient. These entries from a school log-book will show you some of the things that happened:

> The monitors do not improve, the children are forgetting all they know and are exceedingly idle, when I go round the class to examine the writing I find nothing on their slates.

> E. Abrahams has taken the second class this week, they have made no progress in the reading lesson, she taught them 'Teds is key' instead of 'Ted's keg'. She was unable to take the sewing lesson as she cannot sew so well as the children.

> E. Abrahams had not lighted her fire, dusted the room, nor arranged the forms, children crying with the cold.

Edwin Snook kept in by Amy Hallows who went home and forgot him.

Amy Hallows placed Tommy Bird on a high form and tied him there, he fell forward and pitched on his head.

Louisa Love, the monitress, dismissed for having the boys in the classroom and misconducting herself.

In infants' schools even headmistresses were sometimes not very efficient or very well educated. There were, however, many headmistresses who were willing to give good service in return for low salaries. At one time Campbell Square Infants' School was fortunate enough to have as its Head a lady called Marianne Farningham Hearn. She was quite famous in her time as a writer and as a poetess. You can read about her in the 'Dictionary of National Biography'.

THE CHILDREN

How old are children when they enter primary school to-day? How old are they when they leave? You can find these things out for yourself. You will also find that the age limits are strictly followed. Children cannot enter the school under age and they have to leave at the proper time. This was not so in Victorian times. If a child was so backward that he could not attempt the work of Standard I then he stayed with the infants. At least one boy stayed until he was nine. However, it was much more usual to start school very early. One old lady told me she started when she was only two! She was then a rather sickly child and as she lived a long way from school, older girls used to meet her on the way and carry her in relays. Quite a lot of children started school at two, and at least one child started even earlier as is shown by this entry in a log-book:

Admitted a baby fifteen months old.

The reason why children went to school so young is easy to discover. Many families were so poor that the mothers had to

A class of infants in 1891. The teacher has just asked, 'Which is your right hand?' What answers are the children giving her?

go to work, and they packed their children off to school at as early an age as possible.

THE LESSONS

As you would expect, the infants did very elementary work – the beginnings of reading, writing and arithmetic.

They started by learning their letters. Sometimes they had a box of wooden letters; sometimes they had cards with the alphabet on them. The first reading books were called primers. One that I have seen was called, 'A Good Book To Teach Me How To Read'. Like the books used in the boys' school, it makes the mistake of supposing that short words are easy to read. The book starts with two letter words, first in lists, then in sentences. Could you make up a sentence of nine words, each word of two letters only? This is what the primer does! 'Lo it is so as ye go to it.' Other shorter examples are, 'So we go on to it as he' and 'Be ye as he is or as 61 we.' How much sense do you suppose these sentences made to a child of six or seven? Things become a bit easier when the author of the book allows himself to use three-letter words:

No man can see God,
God can see all of us,
Let me go in His way,
It is a sin not to go in it.

Do you think that the ideas here are easy to understand?

In arithmetic the children started by learning to count, and went on to do very easy sums. A favourite way of teaching them was by using the ball frame.

You can count, add up, take away or even multiply and divide by sliding the beads along the wires.

A ball-frame

Some schools economised by letting children use their fingers instead of the ball-frame, but this was discouraged. As one teacher said:

Where children, as infants, are taught to reckon by means of fingers, the practice is continued and they are found in the highest standards, and even as pupil teachers, playing the fatal finger tattoo.

You may remember that in the schools for older children, they sometimes had object lessons. This happened too in infants' schools, except that here such lessons were given regularly. Usually they were very popular with the children. All sorts of things could be taken as objects, such as bread, tobacco, water, leather, elephants, Roman numerals, the clock, the shoemaker and so on.

In the 1880s teachers were beginning to hear about *kindergartens*. These were infants' schools where teachers used the ideas of Froebel. If you find out what the word kindergarten means you will know the kind of place that Froebel wanted a school to be. No Victorian infants' school was as Froebel would have liked, but the schools were brighter places for trying to carry out his ideas. You can see this from a list of toys bought by one school. It included a wheelbarrow,

a watering-pot, four small buckets, a set of cardboard work, a toy tea-set, four dozen counters, two gross of transparent beads and a Noah's ark. On page 63 you can see some playground equipment. Froebel himself would not have liked many of these things. He believed in simple things like balls and bricks, which leave plenty of room for imagination. The two best toys any child can have are sand and water, which helps explain why the seaside is such a popular place.

Infants also did a little needlework. Here the school ran into the problem of paying for the materials, since the infants were unable to make anything worth buying. One solution was to make them use their wool over and over again. As soon as they had finished a piece of knitting, they had to unravel it and start all over again!

Before we leave the infants, here is a problem for you to think about.

Supposing you had a class of fifty or sixty children, how would you keep them all together, still, in one place, so that they could all see and be seen by the teacher? The solution was to use a gallery. This was a sort of grandstand with rows of seats one above another. The children were packed in like sardines, and the teacher stood in front of row upon row of little faces.

8 How Campbell Square School Began

Now that we have a picture in our minds of Campbell Square in 1888, we will go right back to the beginnings of elementary schools.

In 1800, only one child in thirty had a proper education. Everyone thought that it would cost far too much to provide schools for all children. Then two men came forward with an idea. They were Joseph Lancaster, a Quaker, and Andrew Bell, a clergyman of the Church of England. They believed they had solved the problem of giving cheap and efficient education to all the children of England.

In 1803 Lancaster wrote a book called 'Improvements In Education'. In later years he said of this book:

> When I first commenced making known my system of education to the public, I stated that one master could govern a school, however large: that a simple principle of order would enable him to govern hundreds of pupils and thus prepare for their instruction: that one book would teach a whole school to spell, one book for reading and one for arithmetic: that five hundred pupils might write and spell at the same time: and that a boy who knew nothing about arithmetic might, on this system, teach it as well as the master himself.

Can you imagine a school of five hundred pupils with one teacher and three books? Lancaster claimed at another time that on his system one master could teach a thousand pupils. It was thought that the cost would be between 4s (20p) and 7s (35p) a year per pupil. How was this to be done?

A monitorial school in the early nineteenth century

The school was to be split up into small groups. Each would be taught by a monitor. The master would meet his monitors every day before school and teach them what they had, in turn, to pass on to the children. When school began the teacher, in theory, had only to supervise. As monitors earned only a penny or twopence a week, you can see that the system was not expensive.

In 1808, in order to encourage the building of schools, Lancaster's friends formed the Royal Lancasterian Society. However, Lancaster was so difficult to work with that the Society broke away from him. They now called themselves The British and Foreign Schools Society. Schools belonging to this Society were known as 'British Schools' – a very misleading title.

Not to be outdone, the Church of England resolved to start a society of its own. This it did in 1811, naming it The

National Society for Promoting the Education of the Poor in the Principles of the *Established Church*. Andrew Bell became its first Superintendent. The Society called its schools 'National Schools'. This, too, was a misleading title.

The founding of the National Society had some rather unfortunate results for the British Schools. The British Schools taught non-denominational religion, but in spite of this members of the Church of England had been giving money to them. But now the Church of England had schools of its own, and so naturally its members helped them instead. The supporters of the British Schools were the Nonconformists – Baptists, Congregationalists and Methodists.

In Northampton, in 1810, things began to move. Many important people met together and decided to start a British School. This was the very beginning of the Campbell Square

School which you read about in the earlier chapters of this book. The Marquis of Northampton gave £30; other important people gave ten guineas (£10.50) each; others gave as little as five shillings (25p). Altogether 120 people contributed money to start the school, and promised to pay something each year to keep it going. These subscribers elected a few of their number to be managers. The managers were to look after the business affairs of the school, to collect money and decide how to spend it, to appoint a teacher, to pay his salary and see he did his job properly, to buy school equipment and to keep the school building in repair.

However, soon after the opening of the British School, some Church of England people in the town started a National School. Many children and subscribers went over to it, so the British School lost both pupils and money. Fortunately, there was plenty of room for both schools in Northampton, and, in 1816, the British School was well under way. It had over 150 pupils and a good master. The managers said:

> The zeal and ability with which Mr Hall has conducted the School and the attention he has paid to the morals and *deportment* of the children merit our warmest thanks.

To show their appreciation, they gave Mr Hall a rise in salary.

The School also had quite a good income for those days. Here are their receipts for 1814:

Subscriptions	£252	10s 11d (£252.54)
Donations	£12	0s 0d (£12.00)
Charity Boxes	£2	13s 8d (£2.68)

You will also see that all the money was given voluntarily. It was for this reason that schools like the Northampton British School were known as *Voluntary Schools*. Until 1870, all elementary schools were Voluntary Schools.

What was it like in the Northampton British School in those early days?

The building was one enormous room. Down the centre of the room were desks used for writing, while at the sides there were spaces where small groups of children stood for reading. Here is a picture of monitors taking a reading lesson in 1816:

You can see the monitor in charge of each group and you can also see that the children are all reading from the same sheet. This, of course, saved considerable expense in buying books.

They had some rather odd ways of encouraging children to work. Lancaster describes what happened when a child was put up from one class into another:

> The boys who obtain prizes commonly walk round the school in procession, holding the prizes in their hands and a herald proclaiming before them, 'These good boys have obtained prizes for going into another class.'

There were also merit cards. Boys won these for good work and good behaviour. When they had collected enough, they took them to the teacher and exchanged them for cash.

Discipline, too, was peculiar. Lancaster was a Quaker, and as Quakers never use violence, he was against caning. He did advise some strange punishments, though. Boys who misbehaved were made to tramp round and round the schoolroom with heavy logs tied round their necks, until they were too exhausted to play up. Others were tied in sacks, and others put in baskets and hauled up to the ceiling. I think that Mr Hall, the teacher in Northampton, was not as cruel as Lancaster would have liked, but some odd things certainly happened here. Boys wore dunces' caps, or had to wear their coats back to front, while one unhappy lad had to run home through the streets without his trousers.

How much could children learn at these monitorial schools? The answer was: not very much. The people of Northampton, like people all over England, at first supported their monitorial schools with great enthusiasm and thought that they would work miracles. As the years went on they began to have doubts, and the managers sadly reported:

> The Committee have to regret, in common with the friends of education generally, that by far the majority of the Children are taken from the School before they have well acquired the *rudiments of education.*

9 Campbell Square School in 1870

By 1870 great changes had taken place at Campbell Square School.

They had moved to another building. The new school had been opened in 1846. By now the boys' school did not stand alone. A school for girls had been provided in 1846 at the same time as the new school for boys and in 1870 an infants' school was opened.

The cost of the new infants' building was £800. How much does it cost to build a school of average size today?

Apart from the building there had also been important changes among the teachers. The school was now employing pupil teachers.

You will remember reading, at the end of the last chapter, that the managers realised that the school was not getting good results with monitors. This happened everywhere. People slowly began to realise that there could be no good education without properly trained teachers.

One of the first people to grasp this was James Kay Shuttleworth. He had begun his working life as a doctor and was in Manchester at the time of a serious cholera epidemic in 1832. He found that much of his work as a doctor was thrown away because the poor of the town were too ignorant to look after themselves properly or to follow his advice intelligently. He realised that without education, the poor would never be able to live in a better way. This led him to consider how to train teachers. In those days there were not nearly enough secondary schools and training colleges to supply all the teachers that were needed. He found the solution during a visit to Holland, where he saw the Dutch using pupil teachers. Look back to page 11 to remind yourself how pupil teachers worked. On his return to England he tried out the system in a school for workhouse children. It was a success.

Kay Shuttleworth's big chance to work for education came in 1839. In that year the Government set up the Committee of the Privy Council for Education. This was the beginning of the Ministry of Education. Kay Shuttleworth was the Secretary, which meant that he was the chief *civil servant*

James Kay Shuttleworth

in the new organisation. The purpose of the Commitee of Council, as it was known for short, was to supervise the paying of grants which Parliament was making each year to schools. Kay Shuttleworth had to be careful not to introduce new ideas too quickly. In 1846, however, he decided that the time had come. He persuaded the Committee of Council to give extra grants to schools which promised to employ and
72   train pupil teachers.

In spite of the offer of extra grant, the new system spread slowly. Campbell Square, for example, did not have pupil teachers until 1859. Even in 1870 Alfred Jones was still relying mainly on his monitors and had only two or three pupil teachers.

None the less a start had been made. Pupil teachers were more reliable than monitors, but, even more important, some of them became good assistant teachers. Despite all its drawbacks, Kay Shuttleworth's idea worked.

FINDING THE MONEY

There had also been important changes in the finances of the school.

If you compare the school income for 1870 with that for 1814, you will notice several important differences. Here is the combined income for 1870 of all three British Schools in Northampton, Boys', Girls', and Infants':

Subscriptions	£95
School pence	£205
Government grant	£283
TOTAL	£583

You will see that subscriptions were still being paid to the school, but the amount was much smaller and came to no more than a fraction of the total. Happily money had been found in two new ways.

School pence were school fees. The children paid, on an average, threepence (1½p) a week, though big families and poor children paid less and richer people paid more. If Alfred Jones discovered that a parent was an employer, he made him pay sixpence (2½p). Threepence a week for each child may not sound much, but, added together for the year, you will see that the fees amounted to more than twice as much as the subscriptions.

Even more important for the school was the Government grant.

The first grants to schools were made in 1833. They were very small and were intended only to help new schools to pay for their buildings. Later they were given for many other purposes.

But many people were worried about the grants. Accordingly the Government appointed a *Royal Commission* to see how the money was being spent. It was named after its

Robert Lowe

Chairman, the Duke of Newcastle. The Newcastle Commission reported in 1861. The Commissioners concluded that the schools were not doing their job properly. Many children drifted into school, stayed for a year or two and drifted out again. Even when they were supposed to be at school, many stayed away whenever they felt like it. The result was that the teachers concentrated on a few bright children who were willing to attend regularly, while the majority finished their schooldays almost as ignorant as when they began. Many people thought that this was not good enough. Among them

74

was Robert Lowe, the Vice-President of the Committee of Council. He would, today, be called the Minister of Education.

In 1862 he produced what he called his Revised Code. This was a set of rules that schools would have to obey before they could have any grant. Lowe was a hard man. His Code contained some hard rules. When he told Parliament about it, he said that he could not promise efficient education, nor could he promise cheap education. But he did promise that it would be one or the other. If it was not efficient, it would be cheap; if it was not cheap it would be efficient. How did he hope to achieve this? His scheme was 'Payment by Results'. Every year an inspector would visit a school and would give the children an examination in reading, writing and arithmetic. These are the famous Three R's. For every pass in each subject, the Government paid 2s 8d (about 13p), and so a child who passed in all three earned eight shillings (40p) for his school. There was a grant of 4s (20p) for every child who had attended fairly regularly. This meant that a good pupil could earn twelve shillings (60p) altogether.

In 1865 Alfred Jones's results were quite good; 186 boys were examined by the inspector, and 167 passed in reading, 174 in writing and 170 in arithmetic. Thus the grant was almost as high as it could be.

The grants made a big difference to the schools. A good grant meant that the managers had more money to spend on school books, school apparatus and fuel, and on the school building. The grant could even affect the salary of the teacher. A teacher who had good examination results would often ask for extra money, while another who had too many failures might have his salary reduced. It is not surprising that it was hard work preparing for the inspector. Some teachers had rather doubtful methods. One used to stand where the inspector could not see him and signal to his class. Hands behind back meant divide, hands by the sides meant subtract, and so on. But few tried to cheat. Most of them 75 tried to get as many children as possible through the examinations by plain hard work. Instead of spending their time with the bright ones, they concentrated on the others. Children who were somewhat backward had a rather rough time. Schools also offered rewards to successful children. Boys who passed their examinations at Campbell Square received prizes. But Alfred Jones was a kindly man. He wanted to give something to the others who had failed, perhaps through no fault of their own. All he could find, though, was the 'Band Of Hope Magazine' – a religious newspaper.

No one in the schools liked 'Payment by Results'. It could change a school into a sort of factory in which the children were working to earn money for the school rather than an education for themselves. Probably the best thing we can say in its favour is that it may have been necessary a hundred years ago. Even in those days, plenty of people were against it: Kay Shuttleworth was one, Matthew Arnold was another. But in fairness to the government we must remember that by now it was making the biggest contribution to the funds of Campbell Square School and to hundreds of others like it.

10 The Northampton School Board

The following table will show you how fast the population of Northampton grew in the nineteenth century:

1801	11,538	1871	41,168
1821	16,600	1881	51,881
1861	32,813	1901	87,021

This was happening all over England. It meant that the schools were full to bursting. Old buildings had to be enlarged; new schools were needed all the time. Voluntary Societies did their best, especially the Church of England, but they just could not build schools fast enough for the ever-increasing numbers of children.

By 1870 many people had realised that Britain could not afford to go on allowing most of its people to remain without education, especially as many working men had been given the vote in 1868. It was essential to provide a school place for everyone, and since this was too much for the voluntary organisations, some public body would have to do it.

One man who felt this strongly was W.E. Forster. He was a Yorkshire woollen manufacturer who became very interested in politics. He had married the daughter of a famous headmaster, Dr Arnold of Rugby, and thus became brother-in-law to the Doctor's son, Matthew Arnold. Matthew, perhaps better known as a poet, earned his living as a school inspector. It is not surprising that Forster, too, was interested in education.

His chance to provide new schools came soon after 1868. In that year Gladstone became Prime Minister. Forster joined his Government as Vice-President of the Committee of Council for Education.

By 1870 Forster had a Bill before Parliament, and, after a lot of argument, it became law. The whole country was divided into districts. In each district the number of children

W. E. Forster – famous for introducing the 1870 Education Act

had to be counted, together with the number of school places. If there were more children than there were places in the existing schools, the ratepayers of the district were bound by law to elect a School Board. The School Board had to take money from the rates to provide new schools. The object, as Forster explained, was 'to fill the gaps left by the voluntary system'. If there were enough schools in existence, all well and good: a district need not have a School Board. If, on the contrary, there were not enough schools, a School Board must 'fill the gaps'. The new schools were known everywhere as 'Board schools'.

One of the biggest problems to be solved was the kind of religion to be taught in the Board schools. The general opinion was that, since ratepayers of all denominations would help to pay for the schools, it was unfair that the children should learn one form of religion rather than another. Parliament finally adopted the Cowper-Temple clause that 'no religious catechism or *religious formulary* which is distinctive of any particular denomination' should be taught in the Board schools.

You will remember reading about religious instruction in Chapter 6.

How did the Education Act of 1870 affect Northampton? Many people of the town welcomed the idea of a School Board. This was particularly true of the Nonconformists, who disliked seeing so many children going to the numerous Church schools. They felt that some good Board schools would be serious rivals to the Church schools, and provide a good alternative.

So a Board was elected. It held its first meeting in February 1871. Its first task was to count the number of children in the city and to measure the schools, allowing eight square feet (0.74 square metres) of space for each child. It finally decided that the town needed more school places as it had over 2,000 children.

The next move was to provide schools for these children. The Board decided to build two, and at once ran into trouble since it had chosen a site near St Edmund's Church school. The managers protested at once. It was bad enough from their point of view to have Board schools at all, for they taught a kind of religion of which they disapproved, but it was really too much if such schools were to be built on their own doorstep! The Church school managers were afraid that they were going to lose many of their children.

The same kind of dispute went on up and down the country. The Church of England tried to defend its own schools; the Nonconformists encouraged School Boards to build as many as they could. The quarrel was also political, for the Conservatives backed the Church of England, and the Liberals backed the Nonconformists. Unfortunately too many people forgot that, while they were quarrelling over religion, many children were losing their education. This is shown in the 'Punch' cartoon below.

'Obstructives'
Mr Punch (to Bull A 1): 'Yes, it's all very well to say "go to school!" How are they to go to school with those people quarrelling in the doorway? Why don't you make 'em move on?'

In this particular dispute, the Northampton School Board was obliging enough to change the site of one of its schools. The two new schools were completed in 1876. Below you can see the bill for one of them, which includes boys', girls' and infants' departments.

Site	£1,056
Building	£4,050
Fittings	£400
Architect's fee	£300
Extras	£260
TOTAL	£6,066

What would the bill probably be today?

The official opening was a grand affair. All the men who had anything to do with the schools marched through the streets in procession, and had a banquet afterwards. Here is the order of the procession:

Police
Police   Band   Police
Masters
Contractors
Clerk of the Works
Clerk of the School Board; Treasurer
Members of Board
Town Clerk and Coroner
Clerk of the Peace; Registrar
Mace Bearer
Mayor's Chaplain, Mayor, Chairman of the Board
Vice-Chairman;   Ex-Mayor
Aldermen
Town Councillors
Police

I imagine it was a very dull procession. It is also difficult to see why they had to bring the Coroner!

After all this pomp and show, the Board must have felt rather disappointed at what happened when the school opened. Someone complained that children were taking school books away for homework, thus risking losing them; the caretaker protested that some boys had been damaging coats and pulling them off the pegs; an angry parent invaded one of the schools and attacked a pupil teacher!

They seem to have overcome their early troubles, for, in 1878, the inspector reported:

> The two existing Board Schools containing three *departments* each have excellent premises, are well supplied with all appliances for teaching, are regularly visited by the managers and are already producing very satisfactory educational results.

The School Board's work at 'filling the gaps' was by no means over in 1876. The population of Northampton went on growing, and, with it, the need for schools. By 1903, when the Board came to an end, it had built altogether five sets of schools. Everywhere this sort of thing was happening, and in many places the Church of England built as fast as the School Boards. The result was that, when Queen Victoria died in 1901, there was a school place of some kind for almost every child in England. You will remember that in 1800 only one child in thirty could go to school.

SCHOOL BOARD FINANCES

How did the School Board find the money to pay for its schools?

In the first place, it charged school fees. The standard charge was twopence (under 1p) a week, but poor parents were often excused payment.

Secondly, Board schools could earn Government grants. Grants were a very important source of income and paid at least a third of the expenses. The School Board made it clear that the teachers could not expect good salaries unless they earned good grants.

So far, the School Boards were doing what the voluntary schools did, which also charged school fees and earned Government grants. But a voluntary school had to make up the remainder of its income by collecting subscriptions from private citizens. Alas, subscribers sometimes died, sometimes left the district and, quite often, forgot to pay. The School Board was much more fortunate. All it had to do was to work out how much more money it was going to need and to ask the Town Council to pay the amount out of the rates. The Town Council could not refuse. It was bound by law to hand over the money without question. Thus the rates had to go up. This helped to make the School Boards unpopular.

From this table, you can see how the Board's expenditure rose:

1884	£4,500
1890	£6,800
1901	£24,374

CAMPBELL SQUARE SCHOOL AND THE SCHOOL BOARD

By 1870 the managers of Campbell Square School were in difficulties. The building needed altering and enlarging. Alfred Jones had made it clear that he could not run the school properly unless he had extra teachers. Building and extra staff meant extra money. The school was earning good government grants and the children were paying their fees. What, then, had gone wrong? The problem was that people were no longer willing to pay subscriptions to the school. Of course, the managers might have worked harder to raise the money they needed. They might have persuaded people to subscribe, but there was an easier alternative. They could hand over their school to the School Board. Very few managers of Church of England or Catholic schools would have thought of doing this for a moment, as it would have meant that they could not insist on the religious teaching of their choice. However, Campbell Square School was not a Church of England or a Catholic school. All British Schools had given   83 non-denominational religious instruction, even in the years before Board schools. If Campbell Square School became a Board school, its religious teaching would remain the same.

So in 1878 the managers offered their school to the School Board, and the School Board accepted it. At once the school could get extra money, so that the school buildings were soon enlarged and extra teachers were appointed. Of course, the former managers no longer controlled the school, but many felt that it had become too great a responsibility and were glad to escape from their duties.

HOW THE SCHOOL BOARD ENDED

Towards the end of the nineteenth century, secondary schools began to develop. Many of the bright children in schools like Campbell Square School wanted something more than elementary education.

The government was, by now, anxious to encourage them. In many foreign countries, especially the United States and Germany, factories and businesses were growing very fast. These foreign countries were dangerous business rivals. How could Great Britain keep up with them? Most people realised that we needed a good number of well-educated citizens, able to take responsible posts in offices and factories.

The country had nearly enough elementary schools: it now needed secondary schools.

In the 1890s there were already several ways in which a bright lad from a poor home could have a secondary education of some sort or other.

He might win a scholarship to one of the old grammar schools, like the King Edward VI Schools that are found in many towns.

Secondly, if he was lucky, he might live in a town where the School Board had set up higher grade schools. These were schools which took the brighter children from the local elementary schools and gave them some scientific teaching for a year or two.

Finally, there were a few technical schools. These had

been set up after Parliament had passed the Technical Instruction Act of 1889. County councils and county borough councils looked after these schools.

Very few children won scholarships to grammar schools. Most elementary school children who wished to continue their studies had to do so in a School Board higher grade school, if there was one, or in a technical school.

These, however, gave a rather narrow education. They concentrated mainly on scientific and technical work. What many people wanted to see was a new kind of secondary school – one that would teach science, of course, but which also gave plenty of time to subjects like Latin, Greek, modern languages, literature and history.

Who was to have control over these schools? The School Boards had a claim for many of them had started higher grade schools. The county and county borough councils had a claim because they had started technical schools. It was not easy to decide between them.

School Boards, however, had two great disadvantages. First, there were too many of them. Of course the School Boards of towns like Birmingham, London, and even Northampton would have been quite capable of running secondary schools. But there were many small villages that had School Boards – places like Wollaston and Bozeat in Northamptonshire or Radstock in Somerset. A secondary school would have been altogether too much for these little Boards. What was needed was an authority covering a much wider district and the county council seemed the right choice.

Secondly, in 1901, there was a very important legal decision. The Government *Auditor*, T. B. Cockerton, when going through the account books of the London School Board, decided they had been spending their money illegally, by providing higher education. The Act of 1870, he argued, allowed them to give only elementary education. The School Board disagreed. The case was brought before the High Court. The Court had a difficult decision to make, for the Act of 1870 had failed to say what was meant by elementary education.

However, what was clear from the Act was that the School Boards were expected to give an education only to children. The School Board had broken the law in so far as it had spent public money educating young people and adults. This was a blow to School Boards throughout the country.

A. J. Balfour

Probably the most important result of the Cockerton case was that it made a new Education Act necessary. The Government took the opportunity to clear up many educational problems.

The politician who introduced the new Bill into Parliament was A. J. Balfour. Most of the work behind the scenes was done by a junior official at the Board of Education named R. L. Morant.

Balfour thought he was very clever and made him his chief assistant in preference to several more senior officials. His work was so important that the Education Act of 1902 is often called the Balfour – Morant Act.

The Act, together with one of 1903, abolished School Boards everywhere. This was rather like tidying up, for 2,559 Boards were abolished and 330 new local education authorities were created. They were mainly county councils and county borough councils.

One of the most important duties of the new authorities was to encourage the building of secondary schools – the schools that were to grow into grammar schools and later into comprehensive schools.

The Act also made changes in elementary education. You will remember that the Church of England and Roman Catholic schools had been left behind because they had to rely on voluntary subscriptions, whereas Board schools could get money from the rates. In 1902 the Conservative Government was anxious to please its friends in the Church of England. So by the terms of the Act, the Church Schools, too, could have their share of the rates – and go on teaching their own religion. All they had to do in return was to allow the local education authority of their area to choose one third of their managers. The Liberals did not like this. Throughout the country, their friends the Nonconformists were furious at having to pay rates for Church schools. But there is no doubt that after 1902 the Church schools were able to give a better education to the children attending them.

The Act of 1902 meant the end of the Northampton School Board, which held its last meeting in 1903. The Board gave a summary of its work saying it had provided:

1. Well designed and efficient buildings.
2. Better teachers.
3. A more sympathetic atmosphere for the child, and , it   87

is hoped, not a little accomplished towards the making of good citizens, the one great purpose of school training.

The Northampton School Board had worked for over thirty years, with good results for the town. But its task was mainly 'filling the gaps' left by the voluntary schools. The time had come for one authority, with at least some control over all the schools in the town, elementary and secondary. The borough council was waiting to take over this work. The School Board had become old-fashioned. It had to go.

11 Campbell Square School Since 1902

How did the Act of 1902 change Campbell Square School? After 1903 it was called a Council school instead of a Board school, but was allowed to keep its title, British, for some years, until somebody in the Board of Education ordered it to be dropped.

About 1901 people decided that it was time for a new headmaster. Alfred Jones was 72 years old and had been there since 1853. But how do you persuade a man to retire, who does not want to? They decided to drop a pretty broad hint. They organised a dinner-party and gave Mr Jones a gold watch and an *illuminated address*, wishing him a long and happy retirement. Alfred Jones ate the dinner, accepted the gold watch with the address, and announced that he had no intention of retiring. He stayed on as headmaster until 1914!

After 1944 Campbell Square School became a secondary school, but the buildings were already out of date, and unsuitable for modern education. At last, in 1964, Northampton Education Authority closed the school. The buildings themselves were still sound, so they were used as a juvenile court and as offices. The teachers and pupils moved to other schools in the town.

Things to Do

There is no chapter in this book on school discipline. This is something you can write for yourself. In the first place you should hunt through the book and collect all the information you can find. Besides this, I have found in the log-books of schools in Somerset entries which show the ways children misbehaved and were punished. Here are some of them:

A boy gave an immense amount of trouble and would not leave his class when told to do so. The assistant took him by the arms and forced him to leave the room. The elder boys opposed the assistants; the remainder of the afternoon they caused such uproar that work had to be suspended [stopped]; nearly 200 of them held open riot outside the school till after 5 o'clock and when the teachers ventured to leave hooted them home through the streets.

Septimus Drew, caned for disobedience this morning, ran home during play time.

Two boys, William and Arthur Spink, were punished this morning for being so late as to lose their attendance marks. Arthur refused to hold up his hand, and after receiving a few strokes on the back, began to use bad language and make remarks entirely unfit to be heard in school.

Charles was expelled for persistently swearing in class.

Ashman returned to school and promised to reform. In the afternoon he made use of bad language in his class, and when spoken to about it said he should use the same words again if he wished.

Henry Jones was expelled for knocking out a girl's front teeth in the playground.

Wyndham Baskett was insolent and stubborn in his class on Thursday afternoon, and when his teacher's back was turned, left the school without permission. When questioned respecting his conduct he refused to move and was forced to the centre of the Schoolroom where he lay kicking upon the floor until he was confined in a room attached to the School.

While the Master was examining his class, Anneley rose from his seat, and struck Monitor Davis in the face. When the Master went to him and took him by the arm he exclaimed, 'Let me alone you fat-headed fool', called the Master by worse names than this and set the whole school in an uproar. When the Master brought him out he twisted his leg round the table in such a way that he was unable to remove him. Assistant Stevens and Monitor Davis then assisted, Stevens held one hand, the master the other, and Davis his legs. The Master then inflicted four strokes, two for each offence, across the lad's 'terminal vertebra'.

Ernest Pitt and Alfred Fisher were expelled for leading the Scholars of this and Trinity Schools in a mob to attack the Bathforum Scholars with sticks and stones.

Frank Cowley and Henry Giles, both habitual truants, were absent from school again, without leave. They were confined in one of the Class Rooms, and when the master was at tea, one assisted the other to escape by a water pipe, from a window about thirty feet [9 metres] from the ground.

A man named Samuel Woodman entered the school room in a half-drunken state. He refused to leave the room when requested, and used abusive and insulting language to the Master. A Policeman was fetched and Woodman soon left.

A father came into the playground as the boys were marching upstairs, raised his fist and struck at the Master, saying he would knock him down. The Master stepped aside and told him he should prosecute him for the next offence of this kind. He replied that he would knock the master down at any time he struck his boy for any offence whatever.

There is one thing you must remember as you read these stories. They were not the kind of thing that happened every day. As you have seen from reading this book, Alfred Jones kept his school in good order. Most Head Teachers did the same, and these quotations from their log-books only show what happened on the rare occasions that things went seriously wrong.

1. Make a survey of the old schools in your district and mark their position on a map. Also mark the newer schools on the same map and compare their positions.

2. Write an imaginary conversation between a young teacher of the 1880s and a young teacher today, each to describe a day in his life at school.

3. If you decided to become a teacher how would you expect to be educated and trained? What examinations would you have to pass? Compare the modern system with that used for training teachers in 1888.

4. Compare and contrast children's amusements in 1888 with those of today.

5. Imagine a conversation between yourself and a child in 1888. Tell each other about the way you spend your Sunday.

6. Find out by what stages the school-leaving age has been raised. Should it be raised higher today?

7. Find a copy of a small child's reading book. Compare it with the material given on page 41.

8. Find out if there was a School Board in your town. If there was, discover what schools it built. Search the old newspapers in your local library to see if you can find any references to it.

9. Make a rough calculation of the surface area of your school, including corridors and cloakrooms, and find out how many square metres per child you have. Compare this with the space allowed in 1870 (see page 79).

10. Imagine yourself at school in 1888. Write a letter to a friend saying what you think about your lessons.

11. Imagine yourself a monitor in an infants' school in 1888. Describe a day in your life.

12. From the reference books in your school and in your public library, find out more about the following:

Joseph Lancaster	Andrew Bell
James Kay Shuttleworth	Matthew Arnold
Robert Lowe	W. E. Forster
A. J. Balfour	Marianne Farningham Hearn

13. Collect as much information as you can about the old schools in your area. Ask old people to tell you all they can. Visit your local library and ask for information. Study the buildings for dates and inscriptions. Make a scrap-book of your pieces of information.

Glossary

to admonish, to tell someone he or she has done wrong

anaesthetics, a group of drugs which cause loss of sensation: general anaesthetics, such as ether, produce the total loss of consciousness needed for major operations; local anaesthetics make only a particular part of the body lose feeling.

auditor, person employed to check account books and see that they have been properly kept. He/she has to see that there has been no cheating over money

Board School, a school built and maintained by a *School Board*

British School, a school that was a member of the British and Foreign Schools Society. See page 66

Catechism, the system of teaching drawn up in the form of questions and answers

Certificate, in this book it means a document given to a student who has passed a final examination and become a fully qualified teacher

charity boxes, boxes, usually placed in churches, into which people could put money for any good cause they might wish to support

civil servant, person employed by the Government. Most civil servants work in the offices of the various Ministries – War Office, Treasury, Ministry of Agriculture and Fisheries, etc.

compulsory, in this instance it means that the *School Boards* could make children go to schools

consumption, a disease more commonly known as tuberculosis (TB) which usually infects the lungs but can affect any organ

copper-plate, faultless handwriting, used for engraving polished copper

department, a division of a school. In the nineteenth century most big schools would be divided into three departments, Boys, Girls and Infants

deportment, the way a person walks

93

disciplinarian, person (often a teacher) who enforces strict discipline

donation, in this book it means a gift of money made to a school which was not repeated annually (see *subscription*). Donations were often made by will

eczema, a skin disease, in which part of the skin is red with numerous pimples which turn into swellings

Established Church, in England this is the Church of England. The Established Church practises the official religion of a country

fatigue, tiredness

hour-glass, instrument for measuring the hours by running sand through a narrow neck

illuminated address, a handsomely bound folder containing a complimentary message, beautifully lettered and coloured

inconvenience, trouble; making things awkward

indifference, lack of interest

italics, a sloping type of writing or print introduced by the Italian printer Aldo Manuzio in 1501, especially used for emphasis or other distinctive purposes

kindergarten, literally 'children's garden'. In practice it means an infants' school run according to the ideas of Froebel

log-book, a book in which the Head Teacher notes the important events in the life of the school. It was made up weekly or daily. Log-books are valuable sources of information

louver, small turret placed on a roof to cover a hole. This allowed air to pass through, but kept out rain. Louvers can be seen on the roofs of many old schools

monitor, a senior pupil who taught the younger children

non-denominational religion, religious beliefs which Christians agree about, as distinct from beliefs found only in particular religious organisations. For example, all Christians believe that Christ was the Son of God. However, only members of the Church of England and the Roman Catholic Church believe that they should have Bishops

penny miscellany, a comic

profile, the outline of a head, viewed from the side

quarter-day, first or last day of a quarter of a year (i.e. three months), on which rent or interest is paid

religious formulary, a religious belief. The Creed is made up of religious formularies

ringworm, a skin disease which is usually noticed by ring-shaped patches

94

Royal Commission, a body of people appointed by the Government to look into a serious national problem and to suggest some solutions

rudiments of education, the first steps in education. In the last century this meant knowing how to read and write a little and how to do simple arithmetic

salutary, good – from a Latin word meaning 'health'

School Board, a group of people, elected by the ratepayers, who had the duty of building schools in their area if there was a shortage. School Boards were first started in 1870 (see pages 78–9)

skull-cap close fitting, velvet cap worn indoors by old men

subscription, a sum of money given regularly each year by a private person, in this case to a school

substantial interest, in this instance it means plenty of extra punishment

Tonic Sol-Fa, system of musical notation to help make sight-reading music easier. The notes are named doh, ray, me, fah, soh, lah, te

Total Abstinence, never drinking anything containing alcohol

training college, a college for the training of teachers. Students entered when they were about 18 or 20 and stayed full-time for two years

tuning fork, fork about 15 centimetres long, with two prongs and a very short handle. When hit on the prongs and held upright on the table, it will give a musical note. You can get something of the effect with an ordinary dining fork

vaccination, injecting a special preparation of live microbes to give immunity to a disease without causing the disease

Voluntary Schools, schools built and looked after by voluntary organisations. They depended, entirely or in part, on money given by private individuals. Most of these schools belonged to the Church of England

Index